D

Morgan L

based on the novel by Bram Stoker

CW01432542

methuen | drama

LONDON • NEW YORK • OXFORD • NEW DELHI • SYDNEY

METHUEN DRAMA

Bloomsbury Publishing Plc, 50 Bedford Square, London, WC1B 3DP, UK
Bloomsbury Publishing Inc, 1359 Broadway, New York, NY 10018, USA
Bloomsbury Publishing Ireland, 29 Earlsfort Terrace, Dublin 2,
D02 AY28, Ireland

BLOOMSBURY, METHUEN DRAMA and the Methuen
Drama logo are trademarks of Bloomsbury Publishing Plc.

First published in Great Britain 2025

Copyright © Morgan Lloyd Malcolm, 2025

Morgan Lloyd Malcolm has asserted her right under the Copyright, Designs
and Patents Act, 1988, to be identified as author of this work.

For legal purposes the Acknowledgements on p. vii
constitute an extension of this copyright page.

Design concept by Émilie Chen

Photography by Charlie Clift

Bloomsbury Publishing Plc does not have any control over, or responsibility
for, any third-party websites referred to or in this book. All internet addresses
given in this book were correct at the time of going to press. The author and
publisher regret any inconvenience caused if addresses have changed or sites
have ceased to exist, but can accept no responsibility for any such changes.

No rights in incidental music or songs contained in the work are hereby
granted and performance rights for any performance/presentation
whatsoever must be obtained from the respective copyright owners.

All rights whatsoever in this play are strictly reserved and application
for performance etc. should be made before rehearsals to The Haworth
Agency, Studio 103, Babel Studios, 158b Kentish Town Road, London,
NW5 2AG (permissions@haworthagency.co.uk). No performance may
be given unless a licence has been obtained

A catalogue record for this book is available from the British Library.

Library of Congress Control Number: 2025944489

ISBN: PB: 978-1-3505-9246-9
ePDF: 978-1-3505-9248-3
eBook: 978-1-3505-9247-6

Series: Modern Plays

Typeset by Mark Heslington Ltd, Scarborough, North Yorkshire
Printed and bound in Great Britain

For product safety related questions contact
productsafety@bloomsbury.com.

To find out more about our authors and books visit
www.bloomsbury.com and sign up for our newsletters.

This version of *Dracula* was first performed at the Lyric Hammersmith Theatre, London on 11 September 2025 with the following cast:

Cast (in alphabetic order)

Lucy	Mei Mac (she/her)
Jonathan	Jack Myers (he/him)
Mina	Umi Myers (she/her)
Van Helsing / Ensemble	Phoebe Naughton (she/her)
Elsie / Ensemble	Macy Seelochan (she/her)
Renfield / Ensemble	B Terry (they/them)

Creative and Production Team

Written by	Morgan Lloyd Malcolm
Directed by	Emma Baggott
Set & Costume Design by	Grace Smart
Lighting Design by	Joshie Harriette
Composition & Sound Design by	Adam Cork
Movement Direction by	Chi-San Howard
Illusion Design by	John Bulleid & Gareth Kalyan
Fight & Intimacy Direction by	Bethan Clark
Casting by	Heather Basten CDG
Voice Coach	Annemette Verspeak
Casting Associate	Louisa Smith
Assistant Director	Gráinne Flynn
Casting Assistant	Joyce Lulendo
Assistant Movement Director	Ana Iversen
Observer Directors	Harry Daisley, Dubheasa Lanipekun & Kim Wright
Gothic Horror Consultant	Dr Sorcha Ní Fhlainn
Company Stage Manager	Claire Bryan
Deputy Stage Manager	Caoimhe Regan
Assistant Stage Manager	Jack Bond
Lighting Programmer	Dan Miller
Lighting Operator	James Knight
Sound Operator	Scott Bradley

Fly person	Tom McCreadle/Will Collins
Wardrobe Assistant	Elizabeth McAllister
Set built by	Visual Scene
Additional Set Items by	Lyric Workshop
Costume Supervision & Making by	Lyric Costume Department
Lighting equipment supplied by	White Light
Sound equipment supplied by	Stage Sound Services
Rehearsal and production photography by	Marc Brenner
Poster image concept and design by	Émilie Chen
Poster image photography by	Charlie Clift
Programme design by	Hannah Yates

ABOUT THE LYRIC

The Lyric Hammersmith Theatre produces bold and relevant world-class theatre from the heart of Hammersmith, the theatre's home since 1895.

Under the leadership of Artistic Director Rachel O'Riordan and Executive Director Amy Belson, we are committed to being vital to, and representative of, our local community. A major force in London and UK theatre, the Lyric produces adventurous and acclaimed theatrical work that tells the stories that matter.

The Lyric is unique in our combined role as a local theatre serving our community and major national producing house, with a pioneering approach to supporting young people through and into theatre. At the core of our mission and values are the people of West London, who are vital to our work as a theatre. We are committed to working with local partners to create a cultural and creative community that brings people together, attracts visitors and supports the local economy. We bring genuinely eclectic and bold programming to West London. Our programming re-lenses familiar plays that speak directly to specific communities, and a passion to welcome and engage new audiences. The Lyric Hammersmith Theatre has a national reputation for ground-breaking work to develop and nurture the next generation of talent, providing opportunities for young people to discover the power of creativity and to experience the life changing impact of theatre.

We are the creative heart of Hammersmith, proud of our history and ambitious for our future.

STAFF LIST

EXECUTIVE TEAM
Artistic Director
Rachel O'Riordan

Executive Director
Amy Belson

Assistant to the Directors
Megan Gates

ARTISTIC ASSOCIATES
Good Teeth
Tanika Gupta
Nina Steiger
Emily McLaughlin

ARTISTIC TEAM
Associate Director
Nicholai La Barrie

Resident Assistant
Director 2025–26

Birkbeck Placement
Gráinne Flynn

PRODUCING TEAM
Director of Producing and Planning
Chris James

Producer
Kate Baiden

Production Coordinator
Myles Sinclair

Trainee Producer
Layla Chowdhury

YOUNG LYRIC TEAM
Director of Young Lyric
Rob Lehmann

Education Producer
Natalie Jim

Inclusion Producer
Adrian Gardner

Outreach and Partnerships Producer
Alessandra Zavagno

REWIND Producer
Hannah Desai

Young Lyric Hosts
Lanikai Krishnadasan Torrens
Daniela Lucinda Santos
Chiquita Delisser
Amy Whitrod Brown

DEVELOPMENT TEAM
Director of Development
Zosha Nash

Head of Individual Giving
Lina Stein

Development Manager
Francesca Mirabile

Development Officer
Lauryn Thomas

130 Fundraising Campaign Director
Lyndel Harrison

COMMUNICATIONS & SALES TEAM
Director of Communications and Sales
Grace Organ

Senior Marketing Manager
Millie Whittam

Sales and Box Office Manager
Robin Wilks

Press & Marketing Assistant
Mutiat Akamo

BOX OFFICE ASSISTANT (PART-TIME)
Chanel Fernandes

BOX OFFICE ASSISTANTS (CASUAL)
Charlotte Keily
Ellie Bibby
Elliot Aitken
Emer Halton-O'Mahony
Farshid Rokey
Genevieve Sabherwal
James Douglas-Quarcoopome
lydia luke
Mackenzie Larsen
Mara Simão
Talia Kracauer

FINANCE & RESOURCES TEAM
Director of Finance & Resources
Wendy Dempsey

Financial Controller
Charlotte Lines

Accounts and Payroll Co-Ordinator
Lesley Williams

Finance Officer
Kunle Sanni

HR Business Partner
Beverley Dash

Administration Manager
Meghana Shah

Head of Building & Facilities
Brian Elvins

Facilities Manager
Hannah Victory

Maintenance Assistant
Ross Aylward-Tarten

Security Supervisor
Jean-Baptiste Maizeroi

Duty Security
Ilias Sufi
Sam Thompson

Housekeeping Team
Bright Gyau

Feni Wilson
Abdul-Hak Laaraj
Dipesh Sinchuri
Ivan Velinov
Nnamdi Ernest Ugorji
Samuel Anan

PRODUCTION TEAM
Head of Production
Seamus Benson

Company Stage Manager
Claire Bryan

Deputy Head of Production
Elizabeth Dickson

Head of Stage
Will Collins

Head of Lighting
Dan Miller

Head of Sound & Video
Daniel Ronayne

Head of Costume
Harry Whitham

Studio & Events Technical Manager
George Ogilvie

Stage Deputy
Tom McCreadie

Sound Deputy
Scott Bradley

Costume Deputy
Kyle Maenz

COMMERCIAL TEAM
Commercial Director
Paul Gallagher

Bars & Catering Manager
Gareth Chalmers

Events and Hires Manager
Tim Jones

Acknowledgements

Thank you to Chris Haydon for the initial conversations and encouragement and to Rafaella Marcus for your expertise and brilliant mind.

Thank you to Cora Kirk, Sonoya Mizuno, Robert Emms, B Terry, Phoebe Naughton and Suzette Llewellyn for your brilliant work in R&D.

Thank you to Umi Myers, Mei Mac, Jack Myers, B Terry, Phoebe Naughton and Macy Seelochan for always being 'VG'. And to Heather Basten and Louisa Smith for helping us find all of these legends.

And thank you to my partner in screams Emma Baggott and the incredible team you have assembled: Grace, Joshie, Adam, Chi-San, Ana, Bethan, John, Gareth, Annemette, Gráinne, Caoimhe, Claire and everyone else at the Lyric. And, of course, the wonderful Kate Baiden, Nicholai La Barrie and Rachel O'Riordan for taking a leap with the play and giving it this beautiful stage.

Dracula

For the Terrifying Women in my life.

List of Characters

Mina
Jonathan
Lucy
Landlady
Driver
Dracula's Driver
Voice
Mother
Dr Seward
Elsie
Quincey
Holmwood
Van Helsing
Renfield
Creature

Note – if Bernard Hermann could score this that would be the vibe. Or Goldfrapp. Orchestral. Atmospheric.

Staging should be simple and theatrical. Practical effects. Nothing too high tech. Lighting and sound used skillfully. Gothic and Victorian. Of the age.

We should never be completely sure how many people are in the cast. A bit like when the Complicité version of The Chairs *in the late 1990s used body doubles so we couldn't quite understand how they were getting the chairs out so quickly.*

We never clap eyes on Dracula himself. He is a shadow, a presence, he may even be a figment. However he is represented, it is shared amongst the cast.

In the process of making the first production, our ensemble (or 'Acolytes' as we came to call them) were able to decide on the names and histories of the women, trans and non-binary people making this show with Mina. Their names (Elsie Marks, Lu Ming, Danny and Margaret Grace) all come with stories attached, some based on real histories. I encourage future productions to do a similar thing and find names and histories that mean something to the performers embodying them.

It is worth noting also that though there are only four of them in our version this play has the capacity for many more. We were limited to a cast of six but if you have more to play with then there are plenty of opportunities for distributing the roles and populating the stage with many more of Mina's troupe of players.

And finally, the definition of 'women' is always inclusive of trans and non-binary people so please keep this in mind when casting.

BEGINNING

The curtain is down. Snap to darkness. The sound of a wolf howling into the night.

A match is lit. A candle glows. A face illuminated.

This is **Mina**. *She stands in front of the curtain and addresses us.*

Mina   Fear. An emotional response to feelings of threat. Fight or flight or freeze. It can be essential in the survival of our species. It is learnt as well as innate. It is the creeping dread as you strain to hear the sound that woke you at night. It is what tells you to stick to the light side of the street. It is what fuels your disgust and keeps you from tasting something unknown to you. It is what keeps you from stepping too far out of line. It is what keeps you in your place. What we are afraid of as individuals can become collective. And the stories we tell of the beasts that threaten us can make a person's anxiety become a people's fixation.

The stories we tell.

Listen carefully. Beware the teller as much as the tale. We are all afraid of such different things and tonight I cannot promise you will be safe.

But at least we aren't alone.

Ladies and gentlemen. And everyone else. Thank you for joining me this evening. My name is Mina and I know you have come to hear the famous and terrifying story of Dracula as recounted in letters by all those involved. I will do my very best to represent them. However, they were not complete and also at times inaccurate so I hope you will permit me to fill in the blanks. I am the only surviving witness.

There is a loud bang behind the curtain which makes her jump. She does not explain it but ploughs on.

Four women (cis, trans, non-binary) step on stage, waiting. They look at **Mina**.

I am to be assisted tonight by my dedicated friends. They are just as concerned with spreading word of the danger we are all in as I am.

She pauses, as if off script.

Mina   We don't want to have to keep doing this. We're so tired of doing this. But we will continue to tour this presentation to spread awareness. Of what's coming. For us all. For you.

She looks at her followers and says solemnly –

For Lucy.

They nod, bow and quickly exit.

(*To the audience.*) Thank you. Now we are ready to begin.

She blows out her candle and we are plunged into darkness. A loud and ominous note. Music underscores. Filmic and strange.

MINA'S PARLOUR

The curtain rises on a stage that has been inhabited by **Mina** *in whatever way she sees fit for this evening. It is* **Mina's** *canvas.*

Mina   It is my betrothed, Jonathan's journal we must observe first. If we are to do this in order. It was the night before he embarked on his trip.

A loud and sudden bang as a door slams and a man steps in. He walks like a Victorian gentleman but there is something ever so strange about his gait.

Jonathan   I shall be on the first ship out.

Mina   Will you write?

Jonathan   Every day. Will you wait for me, dear Mina?

Mina   Every day.

She holds up her hand and **Jonathan** *stands waiting.*

Mina (*to the audience*)   I shall spare you our insipid goodbyes. I look back on it all now and laugh at how naive we were. I often ask myself what our lives would have been like had he not gone. But if it wasn't him then it would have been someone else. And what was coming for us would always arrive, even if it took a lifetime.

She nods at **Jonathan** *who springs into life.*

Jonathan   Adieu, my darling!

Mina   Adieu!

He leaves.

The decision to marry him was never a hard one. Perhaps I should have thought longer about it. But really it felt like the correct choice. That was how we made such decisions back then. Correctly. The only thing that would ever have given me pause would have been my dear friend Lucy. But she was happy for me . . .

Lucy *rushes on.*

Lucy   I am so happy for you.

Mina (*to the audience*)   You see?

Lucy   He is a good man I think.

Mina   He is.

Lucy   And he will look after you I'm sure.

Mina   It is all we can hope for, isn't it?

Lucy   And love. And romance. And happiness. Can we not hope for that too?

Mina   Perhaps. But we must also be prepared to be content with safety.

Lucy   Remember our riddle?

Mina   Always.

Lucy Not a riddle. A question. Imagine yourself alone in the woods. No weapons. No friends.

Mina Imagine you hear a rustling. You spin round to see who it is.

Lucy You gasp in horror.

Mina You gasp in relief.

Lucy Because who is it you see?

Mina A man?

Lucy Or a wolf?

Mina Who would you rather? Man or wolf?

Lucy (*laughing*) Jonathan or wolf? Answer now, Mina! Jonathan or wolf?

Mina I hope I chose well.

Lucy I'm sure you have, my darling. I wish you all the happiness in the world.

Mina Thank you.

Lucy *kisses* **Mina** *on the cheek and goes.* **Mina** *watches her then turns back to the audience.*

Mina Jonathan or wolf.

Suddenly a loud sound of a ship's horn rings out. We see his journey as **Mina** *speaks.*

THE JOURNEY

Mina He travelled for several days from Munich, through Vienna, past Buda-Pesth. A journey that very much transported him from West to East. He described the population of Transylvania as having four distinct nationalities: Saxons in the south, and mixed with them the Wallachs, who are descendants of the Dacians; Magyars in the west and Székelys in the east and north.

He was headed towards the latter who claim to be descended from Attila and the Huns. He wrote with some level of disdain about the people he met. I am not proud of this. We all still have much to learn about those from foreign climes.

We are now in the Golden Krone Hotel.

Landlady   Welcome! Herr Englishman!

Jonathan   Yes. I'm Jonathan Harker. I have a reservation.

Landlady   Welcome!

Mina   She pulled from her pinafore a letter.

Landlady   For you.

Mina   He waited until he was in his room before he read it.

Jonathan (*reading*)   '*My friend, Welcome to the Carpathians. I am anxiously expecting you. Sleep well tonight.*'

Mina   He would not.

Jonathan   '*At three tomorrow the diligence will start for Bukovina; a place on it is kept for you. At the Borgo Pass my carriage will await you and will bring you to me. I trust that your journey from London has been a happy one, and you will enjoy your stay in my beautiful land. Your friend, Count Dracula.*'

The **Landlady** *reappears suddenly. It startles* **Jonathan**.

Landlady   You must not go.

Jonathan   I'm sorry?

Landlady   Do you know what day it is?

Jonathan   The fourth of May.

Landlady   It is the eve of St George's Day. Do you not know that tonight, when the clock strikes midnight, all the evil things in the world will have full sway? Do you know where you are going and what you are going to do?

She falls to her knees.

Jonathan   I don't know what terrible things you are imagining but I hardly think my work arranging the purchase of property for my client will attract much devilry.

Landlady   Please. Take this.

She stands and pulls a necklace with crucifix from her neck and puts it on him.

Jonathan   You're very kind but I don't need it.

Landlady   For your mother's sake.

She leaves.

Mina   It rattled him. It would rattle me too. The crucifix, the warning, the strange sense that the people here knew more than he did. About what he was headed towards. If only he had turned around and come home right then and there. But he did not.

A carriage arrives. **Jonathan** *loads his luggage onto it watched by the* **Driver** *and* **Landlady**. *A group of people emerge from the darkness and stand watching him wordlessly. It is an eery sight.*

Jonathan *spots them and raises his hand to wave but is clearly unsettled by them. They all in unison make the sign of the cross and then point two fingers towards him. He turns to the* **Landlady**.

Jonathan   What are they doing? What does that mean?

Landlady   It is a guard against the evil eye. Are you sure you want to go?

Jonathan   Yes, of course.

She makes the same sign towards him.

Landlady   May you be safe and return home soon.

Jonathan   Thank you.

He steps into the carriage and leaves. The **Landlady** *and the group of watching people disappear from view.*

CARRIAGE TO THE CASTLE

Jonathan *journeys in the carriage.*

Mina   The journey was fast. The driver whipped the horses mercilessly. They were in a hurry and Jonathan did not know why. And when they reached the meeting place, where he was to transfer into a carriage sent by the Count, there was no one there.

Driver   The Herr should continue to Bukovina with us and return tomorrow or the next day.

Mina   But the horses could sense something. They began to scream.

The sounds of the horses and also of an approaching carriage is almost deafening. It arrives and **Jonathan** *gets out of his carriage with the* **Driver**.

From the new carriage steps an ominous looking figure – **Dracula's Driver**.

Dracula's Driver   You are early tonight, friend.

Driver   The English Herr was in a hurry.

Dracula's Driver   You cannot deceive me. You wished to take him with you when his destination is to my master's castle. Give me his luggage.

Jonathan   Good evening, my name is –

Dracula's Driver   I know who you are, Mr Harker. You are most welcome. I will take you to my master, the Count. Come.

The **Driver** *gets back in his carriage and quickly leaves.* **Dracula's Driver** *ushers* **Jonathan** *into his carriage and they go too.*

Mina   Through the night they went. The sound of wolves following them. Getting closer and closer. Jonathan looked out at the window, straining his eyes for any sight of them, hoping the driver would know what to do. When suddenly, from out of the darkness of the forest it emerged. On the high peak of a mountainous ridge stood a vast ruined castle from whose tall black windows came no rays of light.

The carriage stops and **Jonathan** *steps out. Immediately the carriage goes and he is left looking up at the castle.*

Mina *watches him.*

Mina   He stood alone in the darkness. When I think of how terrified he was . . .

(*To* **Jonathan**.) Be brave.

Jonathan *steps towards the castle.*

THRESHOLD

Mina *watches breathlessly as* **Jonathan** *goes towards the door. He takes it achingly slowly in his fear. But before he can knock, the door creaks open, ominously. As it does we become aware of a looming presence. This is the moment we have all been waiting for. He is here.*

Mina   Jonathan?

She waits as **Jonathan** *seems to process that she is in fact speaking to him.*

Jonathan   Yes?

Mina   Will you speak of what you saw?

Jonathan *timidly indicates towards the audience, acknowledging them for the first time.* **Mina** *nods her assent for him to address them.* **Jonathan** *gathers himself. He speaks as if he is remembering a script.*

Jonathan   Within the doorway, stood a tall old man, clean shaven save for a long white moustache, and clad in black from head to foot, without a single speck of colour about him anywhere. He motioned to Jonathan –

Mina (*interrupting*)   To you.

Jonathan (*correcting himself quickly*)   *To me.* Yes. With his right hand and in excellent English, but with a strange intonation – *Welcome to my house. Enter freely and of your own will.* He made no motion of stepping to meet me, but stood like a statue, as though his gesture of welcome had fixed him into stone.

Mina   The instant, however, that he stepped over the threshold, the Count moved impulsively forward, grasping Jonathan's hand with a strength that made him wince, which was not lessened by the fact that it seemed –

Jonathan   As cold as ice.

Mina   More like the hand of a dead man than of a living man. Again he said –

Jonathan   *Welcome to my house. Come freely. Go safely, and leave something of the happiness that you bring.*

Mina   Oh, Jonathan.

Jonathan *is startled a little by her addressing him like this. It isn't part of the script for him.*

Mina   That wish. Why have I only seen its significance as you repeat it now?

Jonathan   The leaving of happiness?

Mina   Yes. Yes that is it, isn't it? That is what happened to you. To us all. Do you see him now?

Jonathan   Yes.

Mina   Describe him more for them.

Jonathan   He is not how you would come to see him.

Mina   He is never the same for any one person.

The form of Dracula emerges through the following. Whether in shadow or otherwise. He grows.

Jonathan For me he was a strange contradiction. For he looked to be so old that he should not be anywhere but his bed. Or his grave. But he walked like a man of my age. Like his form was lying about what was inside of him. And his features were as strong as he appeared. A thin nose and peculiarly arched nostrils, hair growing scantily round the temples but profusely elsewhere. His eyebrows were massive, almost meeting over the nose, and with bushy hair that seemed to curl in its own profusion. The mouth, so far as I could see it under the heavy moustache, was fixed and rather cruel looking with peculiarly sharp white teeth. For the rest, his ears were pale and at the tops extremely pointed, chin was broad and strong, and the cheeks firm though thin. The general effect was one of extraordinary pallor.

Mina Do not forget his hands.

Jonathan Oh yes! His hands were coarse, with squat fingers. And there were hairs in the centre of the palm. And his nails were long and fine, and cut to a sharp point. And when he leaned over me at supper I could not repress a shudder. It may have been that his breath was rank but a horrible feeling of nausea came over me. He sensed it. And retreated. A smile spread over his face, his sharp teeth protruding over his lips. We fell into silence.

There is a pause as **Jonathan** *believes his part is over.* **Mina** *urges him on.*

Mina Then the wolves . . .

Jonathan Ah yes! I heard them in the valley below the castle. *Listen to them – the children of the night. What music they make!*

Mina He saw in your face how this made you feel.

Jonathan *Ah sir – you dwellers in the city cannot enter into the feelings of the hunter.*

Mina The hunter. You see? The warnings.

Jonathan   I know he isn't here but can you feel him somehow?

Mina *shoots* **Jonathan** *a look. This isn't in the script.*

Mina   What do you mean?

Jonathan   That in telling this we are reawakening him?

This feels like a challenge to **Mina** *and she reacts firmly.*

Mina   That is not possible.

Jonathan   But what if it is?

Mina *stares at him for a moment. A stand off.*

Mina   He is gone.

Jonathan   He feels like he is still with us.

Mina   He is. But not in physical form. You're safe. For now.

Jonathan *seems to crumble.*

Jonathan   Oh god forgive me.

Mina *seems to be desperately trying to keep the presentation going.*

Mina   Jonathan. *You're safe.*

Jonathan   I cannot.

Mina   I know. But you must.

Jonathan   Please. Please.

He shakes and loses his footing. **Mina** *goes and stops him from falling. She signals off for someone and two people come and take him, helping him walk off.*

There is a hushed and whispered conversation between **Mina** *and one of the people. The person hurries off and* **Mina** *takes her place centre stage and gathers herself.*

She opens her mouth to speak and suddenly **Jonathan** *reappears. He looks cowed but resolute.* **Mina** *nods at him and he stares back, slightly panicked, unsure of what to do.* **Mina** *takes the reigns.*

MIRROR

Mina   Days passed with no Dracula as Jonathan was told he had business to attend to. And evenings were spent in his awkward company. Jonathan would work through the paperwork for the houses his firm had purchased in England for the Count. He soon realised this was not to be a quick job. And he had begun to struggle to sleep. And so one morning he rose early, when it was still dark, and decided, he would shave.

A mirror is brought to **Jonathan** *by one of the people.* **Jonathan** *looks a little startled by this. Unwilling to take it at first.* **Mina** *has to step in and make him hold it.*

Mina   He took out his blade and found his travel mirror for there were none in the castle at all. Which had struck him as strange of course. And he was about to find out why they were so absent here. He lathered his face and took his blade to his skin.

Jonathan *suddenly gasps dropping the razor.*

Jonathan   Oh god, what is this, what is this?

Mina   Jonathan.

Jonathan   No, no, no, not me.

Mina   Yes you are. You are alright. This is not real. This is a reenactment.

Jonathan *looks at* **Mina** *panicked.*

Jonathan   It is?

Mina   Yes. And we must continue.

He briefly looks out at the audience but **Mina** *pulls his attention back to her.*

Look at me, Jonathan. It's alright.

He nods and returns to his action.

He lathered his face and took his blade to his skin. Gently doing what he's done so many times before when –

A voice startles us all with its strangeness and volume. Does it come from behind us?

Voice   Good morning.

Mina   He had not expected him because he had not seen him approach in the mirror.

The mirror we have reflects no one except maybe the audience.

Jonathan *reaches up to his neck and realises his throat is bleeding which alarms him. It is all over his hand. He cries out in alarm.*

Mina   Dracula seemed to activate – his eyes flared red, his teeth bared.

Jonathan *panics.*

Mina   He went for his throat but Jonathan drew away which meant Dracula touched the beads which held the crucifix. The change in Dracula was instant. The fury in his eyes were gone.

Jonathan *looks up in relief at this.*

Voice   Take care of how you cut yourself. It is more dangerous than you think. And this is the wretched thing that has done the mischief. It is a foul bauble of man's vanity.

Somehow, inexplicably, the mirror lifts and is seemingly flung across and away. We hear it smash. **Mina,** *who has watched this happen, ducks and covers her head, crying out in fear.* **Jonathan** *runs off in fear.*

Several people step out onto the stage to check on her but don't come near her.

Mina   That was not me.

The people hold their hands up as if to say that it wasn't them either.

Who did that?

They shake their heads then back away, off stage. **Mina** *gathers herself again.*

(*To the audience.*) Forgive me. I have no idea what will occur this evening.

A figure steps onto stage but is so far back and so in the dark we cannot see any features. **Mina** *turns to look at it.*

Who's there?

The figure doesn't respond or move.

Declare yourself if you have intentions. Good or bad.

The figure doesn't respond or move.

I will not be intimidated.

(*Quietly.*) Is it you . . .?

The figure disappears. **Mina** *turns back to us but checks over her shoulder once or twice.*

We have found that in telling this story in so many places we are perhaps opening up some kind of gate. A doorway. To somewhere. We are yet to determine if this is a good or bad thing.

(*She calls off.*) Jonathan? Are you coming back?

She waits and eventually **Jonathan** *walks back on stage.*

Mina   Do you wish to continue?

Jonathan   I do.

Mina   Are you quite sure?

Jonathan   Yes. I am able. For you.

Mina   Tell them.

Jonathan   There is shame attached to what is coming. For Jonathan. For *me*. This part of the story is challenging for a man to admit to.

Mina   Then let me take your shame from you. Shame
implies you had agency when you had none. He and they
took you over. There is nothing more to it. If they were
capable of it themselves the shame would be entirely theirs.
It must always be on them. Say the words I gave you.

CREATURES

Jonathan   He was never around in daylight hours so I
would take the opportunity to explore the castle and I would
find doors locked at every turn. I was a prisoner. Another
time I came across the Count himself making my bed. I
began to understand that there were no staff in the castle,
that he was the only one. It was then that I realised that his
driver was Dracula himself too. He was the architect of
everything I was seeing and experiencing. I needed to find a
way out. And when I asked if I would be permitted to return
home soon, so as to complete our business he said he was not
ready for me to leave yet. In fact he made me write letters
home to say that I was quite well and that I would be staying
longer.

A movement from behind that makes him stop and look. **Mina** *looks
too.*

Jonathan   And then one night I found myself considering
my escape. Leaning out the window of my bedroom and
staring at the courtyard below me. Too high to jump. It was
whilst I let my eyes adjust to the darkness of the night that I
noticed something below me move.

*A strange shape of a creature emerges from the darkness, crawling
vertically down a wall. It moves fast and is hard to see but it is
palpably there. It makes* **Jonathan** *and* **Mina** *retreat to each other
in horror. It will appear like a giant spider but with only four
limbs. It will be monstrous enough to unsettle us.*

Jonathan   What manner of man is this? What manner of
creature? I knew it was him somehow. I watched it scuttle

away out of sight. Towards the woods. And knowing that he was no longer in the castle I decided I had to use the opportunity to explore more of it than I had dared to do so as yet.

Jonathan *lights a lamp and sets out into the darkness of the castle. We can only see him.*

I tried all the doors but they were locked as expected. At last I found one door that gave under pressure. And inside I found –

A bedroom. A large, welcoming bed. A huge swathe of curtains.

I could not help but climb up on it. Lie down. And let the feeling of sleep wash over me.

He has placed the lamp on a side table and is asleep on the bed. We watch him a while, waiting. The light in the lamp begins to flicker. Then it burns suddenly brightly before extinguishing completely. We are plunged into darkness. We wait.

Suddenly there's movement. Three figures approach in the dark. We see them climb onto the bed. Too dark to make them out fully but they move in a strange way, their limbs somehow too long for their bodies. Their movements too jerky to be human. They quickly overwhelm him, like insects with their prey.

Just as they seem about to attack he wakes and screams out in horror. He fights with them, a frantic action of limbs and the terrible noises that the creatures are making. Until suddenly –

Voice   HOW DARE YOU TOUCH HIM?

The creatures are flung backwards as if hit by something bigger than them. They shriek out as they fall.

HE BELONGS TO ME!

Jonathan   I backed away from the creatures. For the first time feeling more safe with the Count than I did with them. But I could see they were not satisfied and feared they would still attack. But it was then that he threw a large hessian bag to the floor in front of them.

A hessian sack falls from the sky with a sickening thud.

It moves, there is something inside it.

There's something in it. It's moving!

From the sack comes the sound of a crying child.

My god. My god!

The creatures descend on the sack in a crescendo of shrieks and building noise as they rip and tear at the baby. It is horrifying and **Jonathan** *falls back on the bed unconscious. Darkness descends.*

ESCAPE

A light flickers and illuminates **Mina** *again. The horror of the previous moment still dissipating.*

Mina   It was several weeks of entrapment after that. He once tried to get letters out by throwing them from the window but the Count found them and destroyed them. One night he tried to get the attention of local travellers who approached the castle. They ignored his cries. Instead focusing on their task of delivering several wooden boxes. Caskets. Another night he was woken by the sound of screams from outside his window. Looking down he saw a woman in the courtyard below.

A woman enters.

Mother   Monster! Give me my child!

Mina   Somewhere overhead the sound of the Count calling out to the woods beyond. Then the wolves came. There was no cry from the woman and the howling of the wolves was short.

We see the woman become overwhelmed by wolves and dragged away.

Jonathan *stands looking deflated.*

Mina Go on.

Jonathan I could not pity her because I knew that with her child dead she was better off dead herself.

I tried every conceivable way of escape. And one day I managed to climb from my window and use a ledge to reach the Count's own room. But it was empty.

Mina He looked for a key but could not find it anywhere.

Jonathan But I did find a door I had not seen before. Leading from his bed chamber down to the very base of the castle.

Mina Once he reached the bottom he found himself in an old ruined chapel. The ground recently dug over. The boxes brought by the locals stacked and filled with earth.

Jonathan I went further down still, into the vaults below the chapel and it was there that I found . . .

Mina Him.

Jonathan In one of the coffins. Asleep.

Mina But with his eyes open.

Jonathan But they were stony, with the glassiness of death.

Mina He fled from there back to his chamber.

Jonathan I sent a letter at this point.

Mina Your final one.

Jonathan It was a mess.

Mina You told of seeing the Count. It made little sense.

Jonathan And after that he came to me. Said he was to leave for England the next day. I asked to leave myself that night. He flung the doors open and in the night air I heard the familiar sound of the wolves.

Wolves howling.

I conceded that I would wait until morning. And in the night I heard him promise those creatures that once he was gone they could have me.

The sound of the creature returning. Limbs start to encroach on the stage.

Are they here?

Mina No.

Jonathan I can hear them.

Mina You are remembering them.

Jonathan That is not possible because I am not Jonathan.

Mina No. But in your presentation of Jonathan you are remembering them.

Jonathan No, I am hearing them. For real. *I hear them.*

Mina Yes. Because we are telling the story of them.

Jonathan Are you conjuring them?

Mina No.

Jonathan So why do I hear them?

Mina Because you are Jonathan.

Jonathan I don't like this. I don't remember saying I would do this. I don't know how I'm doing this.

Mina You agreed. Readily. Do you not remember?

Jonathan No.

Mina You were adamant you wanted to help.

Jonathan I was?

Mina Yes. You said this was important to you.

Jonathan *shakes his head in confusion.*

Mina   We're all as frightened as you are. But it *is* important.

Jonathan   Yes, I suppose it is.

Mina   We have to do this.

Jonathan   Alright.

Mina   Do you need another break?

Jonathan   No. No, carry on.

Mina   Alright. When daylight came you went in search of them, didn't you?

Jonathan   Yes.

Mina   Back to the vault. And there he was again. In his coffin.

Jonathan   But he was changed.

Mina   How so?

Jonathan   He looked younger. And full. Specks of blood on his chin. He had clearly fed well the night before.

Mina   On who?

Jonathan   Not me.

Mina   And you took your chance, did you not?

Jonathan   I did. I found an axe and approached his coffin. Raising the blade above my head, preparing to strike when suddenly – he looked directly at me. My hand slipped. The blade only hit above his forehead, causing a gash but not enough to kill him. And that's when he smiled at me. And I knew. I was not going to be the one to stop him. I had failed. I fled from the vault and hid.

(*Suddenly out of character.*) He had a chance. He could have done it then. The fool! The pathetic fool!

Mina (*firmly*)   Sounds of carts and horses. The coffin being hammered shut. And staring out the window you saw –

Jonathan *shakes himself back into the performance.*

Jonathan   The many wooden boxes of earth, one containing the Count, being taken from the castle.

Mina   And you were alone.

Jonathan   Except for those creatures that he had promised me to.

The sound of the creatures. Their legs and scuttling approach.

I could not stay.

The creatures are getting closer.

I had to escape. My only way out was the window. I secured a rope. I did not know if it was long enough.

The creatures are visible now and fully upon him.

I thought only of Mina as I threw myself into the night.

The creatures' shriek reaches a crescendo as they surge towards the audience. Just as they are about to leap from the stage the lights black out and there is a terrible scream and thud.

ARRIVAL

Lights up on **Mina** *alone in her parlour again.*

Mina   Jonathan was the first person I loved to be a victim of Dracula. He would return to me though. The second person was not so lucky. And I wish to be so very careful about how I tell you of what happened next. I fear that, as with so many stories about my gender, there will be misapprehensions, assumptions, judgements. I hope that you will hear this story as a tribute to a woman who did not deserve the fate she received. And yet also, somehow, became for a short time, beyond monstrous into something else.

I am jumping too far ahead. Giving away the game. She would not approve. I speak to you of my dearest friend Lucy.

The figure of a woman stands with her back to us. Blair Witch style. Ominous.

Who should still be alive today. If we had only known to look for the omens and signs. If we only knew what the threat was. Instead, we were women basking in the joy of courtship and love.

SUITORS

*Suddenly **Lucy** springs onto the stage from a different direction to the strange figure which is suddenly gone.*

Lucy   Mina! You will never guess what happened to me today. A whole life time I have lived without a single proposal from a suitor and in one day I've had not one, not two but three!

Mina   Who?

Lucy   First it was dear Dr John Seward.

Mina (*to the audience*)   Who worked at a local asylum and had a patient that would become incredibly important to our story.

Lucy   Then it was Mr Quincey P. Morris, an American from Texas.

Mina (*to the audience*)   Whose sacrifice will be forever remembered by me in the most permanent of ways.

Lucy   And I needn't tell you of number three, need I?

Mina   Arthur Holmwood!

Lucy   Yes!

Mina   And you said yes to him?

Lucy   Of course I did! I love him so much.

Mina   And you're quite sure?

Lucy   Of course! Why would you ask such at thing?

Mina   My darling, I'm happy for you, but Lucy, this is for life. You barely know him. Or any of them really. You cannot know what he would do for you, do to you –

Lucy   I don't know what you mean.

Mina   No. I. See, I'm conflating –

Lucy   What are you doing?

Mina   I'm conflating a thought from ahead.

Lucy   Pardon?

Lucy *turns to look off, shrugging at someone we cannot see.*

Mina   I'm sorry, I'm getting confused. I'm muddling things.

Lucy   What do you mean 'ahead'?

Mina   I mean I am trying to tell this story and I am worrying about something that I was not worried about at the time. This did not happen, did it?

Lucy   I believe the conversation was *a lot more jolly.*

Mina   I just wished better for you, I guess.

Lucy   You cannot change what happened.

Mina   I know. But also. In another story you would not have had the end that you did. You perhaps wouldn't have married Arthur even. Perhaps you and I could have taken some time to travel. See more than just our little corner of the world. Perhaps we could have asked for more. But that is it, isn't it? That is what this is about after all. We had no choices. We had no other way. And that cannot continue.

Lucy *stares at* **Mina**, *unsure what to do.*

Lucy   But. Are we continuing?

Mina   Yes.

Lucy   Do we just carry on as before?

Mina   You're not even her.

Lucy   Sorry?

Mina   Why is this affecting me so much now? I should not be having this reaction –

Mina *turns abruptly and wanders off, muttering to herself.* **Lucy** *looks offstage for guidance. A couple of people step on briefly and gesture for her to continue.*

Lucy (*faltering*)   I am very very happy and I don't know what I have done to deserve it.

I must only try in the future to show that I am not ungrateful for all god's goodness to me in sending me such a lover, such a husband and such a friend.

She stands a moment. Waiting. Then runs off.

THE FIRST OMEN

Suddenly one of the women, **Elsie***, rushes on dressed a little like* **Mina***. She goes to a phonograph and sets it off. We hear the voice of –*

Dr Seward   My name is Dr Seward and I cannot eat, cannot rest, so I shall diary instead. Since being rebuffed by Miss Lucy I am struggling to find a purpose in my life so I shall have to throw myself into my work.

I have been studying one particular patient for several weeks now. He is a strange case.

Elsie *stops the phonograph.*

Elsie (*to the audience*)   The first omen. Yes! This was it.

She steps forward.

If you piece together the different things that happened around the arrival of the threat then this would be one of those indicators, those signs, of something coming. There is always a sign, is there not? There are always clues. Not always subtle. And we as a people will always have those that see them and call out. Shout out that we should heed them. But no matter how loud we shout. No matter how many times we point at what is clearly happening to so many of us and warn that it is only a taste of what is to come – we will be told we are overreacting. That we are ruining the party. That we are wrong. And they will not listen until it is too late. This was one of those signs.

She sets the phonograph off again.

Dr Seward   His name was R. M. Renfield. Sanguine temperament, great physical strength, morbidly excitable, periods of gloom ending in some fixed idea which I cannot make out.

Elsie (*to the audience*)   If only I had known of him earlier. It's only later that we would see a connection.

Dr Seward   He keeps pets. At first his hobby was to catch flies so as to feed them to his spiders. But when I told him he was to get rid of the spiders he ate the flies himself and then tempted in birds to eat the spiders. However, it was not long before he began to eat the birds also.

Mina *suddenly walks onstage.*

Mina   Sorry. I'm so sorry.

Elsie *looks at her waiting for instruction.*

Mina   It feels strangely different tonight, don't you think?

Elsie   Does it?

Mina (*softly to her*)   Yes. I can feel her.

Elsie   Do you wish to stop?

Mina   No.

Elsie   I can continue in your place. I know it well enough.

Mina   No, I must do it. Thank you.

She nods to **Elsie** *who bows slightly and rushes off stage.* **Mina** *looks back to the audience and jumps straight back into the performance.*

Mina   My god if only we had known. And it was not long until the next omen came –

THE SECOND OMEN

The sound of a huge storm at sea. Waves crashing. Lightning. Wind.

Mina (*yelling over the sound of the storm*)   I stood atop the cliff at Whitby and watched as a ship was tossed in the waves. She did not seem in control of herself. In fact, there seemed to be no one at the helm. That was until we saw him. The form of a man. Tied to the wheel. The ship came to a halt in the harbour steered by a dead man. He must have fastened the knots with his teeth. You see the schooner was Russian, from Varna and was called the Demeter. Its main cargo was a great many wooden boxes filled with soil and mould. These boxes. You see? And not just that but from the ship leapt a large black dog. That dog. Don't you see? That dog!

Suddenly the storm stops.

I was not on the ship. I do not have first hand knowledge. But we do have the ship's log.

She goes to a drawer in a cabinet and pulls it open. Reaching in she pulls out a large book.

I think it is important you know what happened on there. It is an important if terrifying part of the story.

She looks off stage.

Yes?

A crowd of sailors rushes on.

Ready?

They nod then assembled themselves.

Just do as you hear. As you ever do.

THE DEMETER

*The parlour changes once again. They stand on the deck of the
Demeter. As* **Mina** *reads the ship's log we see a version of what
happened play out.*

Mina   Sixth July set sail. East wind, fresh. Crew – five
hands. Eleventh July, at dawn entered the Bosphorous.
Boarded by Turkish customs officers. All correct. Thirteenth
July, passed Cape Matapan. Crew dissatisfied about
something. Seem scared, but would not speak out.

Fourteenth July. Anxious about the crew. They still won't say
what is wrong. They just say there is *something* and cross
themselves. Sixteenth July, Mate reported that Petrofsky is
missing.

We lose one of the crew.

Crew downcast. All insisting there is *something* on board with
us. Seventeenth July, Olgaren came to my cabin and
confided in me that he has seen a strange man aboard the
ship. A tall, thin man.

The shadow, a looming image of the tall thin man.

Ordered a search of the whole ship but no sign. Twenty-
fourth July, another man lost.

We lose another crew member.

Men all in panic of fear. Twenty-eighth July, four days in
hell, knocking about in sort of maelstrom, the wind a
tempest. No sleep for any one. Twenty-ninth July, another
tragedy, another gone. Second Mate.

We lose another crew member.

Thirtieth July, near England, awakened by Mate to tell me both man of watch and steersman is missing.

We lose two more crew members.

Only myself and Mate and two hands left to work the ship. First August, two days of fog. We seem to be drifting to some terrible doom. Second August woke at midnight to a cry.

Could see nothing in the fog. One more gone. Lord help us!

We lose another crew member.

Third August, at midnight I went to relieve the man at the wheel but when I got to it found no one there.

We lose another crew member.

The wind was steady and I dared not leave it so shouted for the Mate. He arrived, wild eyed, and whispered hoarsely –

First Mate   IT is here; I know it now. On the watch last night I saw It. Like a man, tall and thin and ghastly pale. It was in the bows and looking out. I crept behind It and gave It my knife but the knife went through It, empty as the air. I'll find It! In the hold perhaps in one of those boxes. I'll unscrew them one by one and see. You work the helm.

Mina   And I could not leave the helm. I heard the Mate banging and hammering in the hold. But then suddenly this stopped and there was a piercing scream and he came running to me.

First Mate   Save me! Save me! Come with me! Before it's too late! The sea will save me from Him. It is all that is left!

He throws himself overboard.

Mina   Fourth August, still fog. I dare not leave the helm. And in the dimness of the night I saw It –

Him! I should have jumped overboard but I am the captain and I must not leave my ship. I shall tie myself to the helm and I will wait. If we are wrecked, mayhap this log may be found and those who find it may understand; god and the blessed Virgin and the saints help a poor ignorant soul trying to do his duty . . .

She puts the ship's log down.

We buried the ship's Captain on the tenth of August. And it was only the next day when it began for dear Lucy. What horror had arrived at our shores?

The light goes.

LUCY

*We hear **Mina**'s voice but it is too dark to see her.*

Mina   I woke in the night. Pitch black but I knew something was wrong.

*She is transported into the bedroom of the lodgings she and **Lucy** share in Whitby. Two beds. She is in one and the one next to her is empty.*

Mina   Gone. She was gone. I got up quickly and checked the house but saw that the front door was open. I grabbed a heavy shawl and ran out into the night.

She runs through Whitby.

I ran to the cliffs first, our favourite bench. Then looking up I could see the silhouette of the church on the horizon. Somehow I was drawn to it. As I reached the graveyard I could see something ahead of me moving.

A mass moves in the darkness.

This is where I wish to stop and explain so many things about Lucy and who she was.

How she was funny and silly and kind. How she loved the colour green and every day would have a new interest. How from one day to the next she would surprise you with new things to talk about. Art, ghosts, animals. How she loved

talking about what she was scared of. The nightmares that
would plague her as a child. That despite them she was
somehow never scared of being scared. How she read books
hungrily and had one of the sharpest minds I know. And
sometimes, when I was sad, she was the only person I would
want to be with. Because she would make me feel safe.
Because she would let me just lay my head on her lap and
cry and she wouldn't try and stop me or tell me how to feel
better. She was not afraid of unbridled emotions. And she
knew me the best in all the world. Even better than
Jonathan. And there were times when we would be together
that we felt like one body not two. So entwined were we.

She was essential to me in a way I cannot describe. And I
really need you to know that before I tell you about what
comes next. Because it matters.

*She pauses a moment, looking out, hand to her eyes as if she can see
something, or someone, in the auditorium.*

Hello? I see you, I think. No, don't go!

*The slam of many doors in the auditorium as whoever she saw
disappears.*

Damn.

*When **Mina** turns back we can just about make out that **Lucy** is
lying on the bench, back arched, clothing ripped, arms reaching up
and a strange smile on her face. Then we see in the shadows
something is on top of her and it raises its head. **Mina** screams in
terror and runs towards her. Whatever the creature is disappears.
Mina wraps **Lucy** in her shawl, fastening it with a safety pin. They
return home and **Mina** helps **Lucy** into bed.*

Mina *cradles* **Lucy**.

Lucy   Please don't tell mother.

Mina   I won't.

Lucy   I did not want to go.

Mina   I know.

Lucy   He took me.

Mina   Who did?

Lucy   Don't judge me.

Mina   Lucy, you are half asleep. So am I. You must have walked there and got yourself confused.

Lucy   Did you not see him?

Mina   I don't know what I saw. I thought perhaps a dog? I was about to shoo it when it went. You were deep asleep when I got to you.

Lucy   He was no dog.

Mina   Hush now. You need to rest.

Lucy   I'm sorry. I'm so sorry. I feel so ashamed. Will you forgive me, my love?

Mina   The shame is not yours to feel. There is nothing to forgive. Sleep now.

Mina *strokes* **Lucy***'s hair and in moving it off her face uncovers her neck.*

Mina (*to the audience*)   It was then that I noticed what I thought was an injury I had caused. The pin I had used on the shawl. I assumed I had pierced the skin on her throat. I hugged her closer. But nothing I did would have been able to save her. The die was cast. It had begun.

Mina *leaves* **Lucy** *in bed.*

REGRET

Mina   Jonathan?

Jonathan *arrives.*

Jonathan   Yes?

Mina   I think we have reached the moment we reunify.

Jonathan   Yes.

Mina   But tonight I want to stay on Lucy. I don't want to leave her again.

Jonathan   Right.

He turns to leave.

Mina   Wait.

He turns back.

Does it make sense to say that I still blame myself for staying away so long when I could have been here. I could have seen the signs, I could have helped.

Jonathan   You are asking me this?

Mina   Yes.

Jonathan *looks out at the audience, panicked.*

Jonathan   I don't know what I'm supposed to say.

Mina   There is no script for this. Say what is in your heart.

Jonathan   I am empty.

Mina   Jonathan. Look at me.

He is staring out at the audience, breathing hard in panic.

Look at me.

He turns to look.

You are Jonathan.

He shakes his head.

You are Jonathan and you will answer me.

He nods.

Go on.

Jonathan I don't know how much you could have done. Several, grown, capable men were unable to save her.

Mina I could have.

Jonathan If you wish to torment yourself with this thought then you go ahead.

Mina Jonathan would not have said that.

Jonathan What would he have said?

Mina He would not have wanted me to torment myself. But I wish I had been able to stop what happened to her. Despite everything that I know now. I wish she had not had the end that she did.

Jonathan You have regrets.

Mina Of course.

Jonathan A weakness.

Mina He would never have said that either.

Jonathan *looks at the audience again.*

Jonathan I don't know what you're wanting me to say.

Mina Yes you do.

Jonathan Maybe we should stop. You seem confused. Out of your depth maybe. All this is too much for you perhaps. I feel somewhere deep down that you need me to say this. Yes. This is it. That you need me to take you in hand even. You need me to take over and figure all this out. That is what I should do. Hand this to me, Mina. You've done quite enough now. I'm in charge now.

Mina *regards him. An awkward pause.*

Mina (*cold*) What did you say?

Jonathan I said you seem confused.

Mina Are you sure it is me that is confused?

Jonathan   Pardon?

Mina (*furious*)   Because you seem to have lost your way entirely. You don't even know who you are. Pathetic man.

You speak as if you have any kind of power in this space that I have created. That is mine. How dare you think you have any authority to challenge me. I brought you here. Never forget that.

Jonathan *cowers at her sudden rage.*

Mina   When you know the importance of what we are doing. For everyone. For the whole human race. How dare you speak with such dismissive insolence. I am telling this story as I have done for so long and I will tell it as I need to. You will follow my lead and you will do as I command, do you understand me?

Jonathan *is frozen in terror.*

Mina   I asked you – do you understand me?

Jonathan *nods.*

Mina   Then you will do as I tell you. And if I wish to change the way I want to tell this story then I will.

She goes to leave but stops. **Jonathan** *freezes.*

Mina   But.

She seems frozen in thought. She turns back to Jonathan. She considers him. Angry.

Mina   When I came to find you. In the hospital. That was where I realized what was happening.

Jonathan *nods.*

Mina   So we will tell this part. But quickly.

NUNS

Jonathan   You found me in a hospital run by nuns in Buda-Pesht. I had been delirious for six weeks. It was there that you read my account of Dracula's castle. And there that you agreed to marry me straight away.

Mina   But more importantly, I read your account of the events at Dracula's castle. Because it was in reading this that I began to understand. Began to see the signs. Understand the threat. Realise what Lucy had been through. Why she was as ill as she was. And that was when we travelled back.

Jonathan   Yes. You were quite frantic.

Mina   I was so angry with myself for not seeing it sooner. And immediately wrote to my friend, Van Helsing. Who I knew was someone who could help. Because they would be able to tell us exactly who the threat was. They would reach Lucy before us. They would be able to assist the men. And it was while we were still travelling back that they tried.

Back to Lucy.

She dismisses **Jonathan** *who scuttles off.*

BLOOD

Lucy's *bedroom.* **Dr Seward**, **Quincey** *and* **Holmwood** *are all rolling up their sleeves in preparation for providing a blood transfusion for* **Lucy**. **Lucy** *lies in bed, pale.*

Mina   They all professed to love her. They did love her, I suppose. Not like I did but they were willing to do what they could to save her. But they were limited to human means and what she was suffering from was not a human problem.

She looks at the assembled team behind her, ready for the next bit but looking a bit trepidatious. She turns back to the audience.

It is at this moment that I require you to suspend your disbelief even more than you already have. For we have limited members of our group and we must meet more men than we can represent. Forgive us.

She indicates to her helpers and they spring into action. **Van Helsing** *kicks things off.*

Van Helsing   Gentlemen. There is no time to be lost. She will die for sheer want of blood. We must do a transfusion at once. Who will it be to give their life blood to her?

Dr Seward   I am the youngest and strongest.

Quincey   I may not be young but I am stronger.

Holmwood   I am her intended. It should be me.

Van Helsing   We need not turn this into a pissing competition. You can all help her. God knows she will need more than just one.

Holmwood   Then let it be me first.

The other two men step aside. The blood transfusion occurs.

Mina   It was sweet of them, I suppose, to try. But though their hearts were in the right place I fear they were simply treating the symptoms and not the cause.

Lucy *revives.*

Lucy   Arthur?

Holmwood   I am here.

Lucy   What happened?

Holmwood   You were quite ill, my darling. But I gave you my blood.

Lucy   I feel so much better.

Holmwood   I would do anything for you.

Lucy   Oh, Arthur.

Dr Seward   We all would!

Light falls, **Lucy** *lies back to sleep, the moon comes out. Over which –*

Mina   And night would come. And though they would resolve to watch her, inevitably they would sleep and whilst they did, Lucy would be visited again. Large wings beating at the window. Lucy, unable to resist, would let him in.

Lucy *throws open the window and is enveloped by a dark creature. The creature leaves. The sun rises.* **Lucy** *is pale and empty again.*

Van Helsing   My god! There is no time to be lost! She needs a blood transfusion!

Dr Seward   Let it be me this time!

Holmwood   We must begin!

Quincey   Hold her down!

Mina   The sheer force of their actions, the insistence. I would wonder for years if she could feel this. If she was aware of what they were doing. If she would have chosen it, if asked.

The blood transfusion happens. **Lucy** *revives.*

Lucy   What happened?

Holmwood   Dr Seward's blood revived you this time.

Lucy (*to* **Dr Seward**)   You are my hero.

Dr Seward   I would do anything for you.

Quincey   As would we all.

Van Helsing   Dear Lucy.

Lucy   You are all my heroes.

The men preen. **Mina** *rolls her eyes.*

Mina   Good grief.

Over the following **Lucy** *goes back to sleep, the moon returns, the creature returns.*

Mina   I can only rely on what was written in their journals.
That I do not believe Lucy spoke like this considering how ill
she was, is of no consequence and I will of course report
what was written. But seriously? And my friend Van Helsing?
They saw the bite marks and declared they needed time to
consider. To study their books. Such precious time lost when
they should have known instantly. With everything I had
told them in my letter.

With the blood lost. With the puncture marks in the neck.
How did they not know?

Lucy *falls back to the bed, drained. The creature leaves. The sun
rises.*

Van Helsing   My god! There is no time to be lost!

Dr Seward   She needs another blood transfusion!

Quincey   It is my turn to give her the blood of life!

Holmwood   Let us not hesitate!

Blood transfusion. Over the following the men, as before, leave
Lucy *alone and the creeping dread of what is coming approaches
and takes* **Lucy** *over.* **Mina** *controls this change in tone.*

Mina   And forgive us for making light of this situation. It is
only to provide respite for us all before what is to come.
Because I want to bring you back to the truth of the
situation. For Lucy. For I wish to note how he came to her.
Because it seems to matter how we each see him. Jonathan
saw an ancient man, jagged teeth, hirsute, smelly, long nails.
He never said it in his journals but the way he described him
was familiar to me. For it was not dissimilar to how he would
describe his late father. I am not saying his father became
Dracula. But perhaps Dracula became his father in some
way. An echo.

Night falls, the creature comes.

And for Lucy? She would expect him at the window. Wings
beating against the glass. A bat-like creature. Who would

become a man and devour her. And if I know anything about that girl I grew up with it was that as a child she would wake from nightmares most nights and talk of swarms of bats. A cloud of them above her, threatening to overwhelm her. The one thing that broke through her barriers. Fear. It lives in us all. It is unique to us all.

*Day comes, ***Lucy*** is drained. When the men speak it is with none of the comedy of before. It is with regret and horror.*

Van Helsing   My god. She is dying.

Holmwood   Lucy!

Quincey   I can provide more blood.

Dr Seward   Her vitals are so low.

Mina   And yet sometimes when she would wake, screaming from her nightmares, she would be sweaty with desire for them to come and take her away.

Lucy *suddenly rises up in bed screaming. Her eyes are red, her teeth are long and sharp. She stands towering over the men.*

Lucy   Take me! Take me now! I am ready to be free of this world. I am ready for release from this life. This pathetic, half life. Release me from these chains. These jailers. Locking me down. How dare you touch me? How dare you even think you are worthy of me? Filling me up with your filthy blood. You think you know what my body needs. What it is capable of. You think you can save me. From what? From who? It is not me that is in danger, it is you. You are no match for me. For you can destroy my body but you cannot destroy who I am. I am beyond the human form. And I will take you. I will have you like you would have me. Come to me.

*With a sharp twist of her neck she turns to look at ***Holmwood*** and smiles.*

Lucy   KISS ME.

Van Helsing *pulls* **Holmwood** *back.*

Van Helsing   Not for your life! Not for your living soul and hers. Do not kiss her.

She lunges forward which makes the men yell out in fear but she seems to lose her power and falls back on the bed. **Van Helsing** *goes to her.*

Lucy   Please. Guard him and give me peace.

Van Helsing   You may kiss her now.

Holmwood *goes to* **Lucy** *and kisses her on the forehead.*

As **Mina** *speaks the following she goes to* **Lucy** *and she rises up to respond to her physically. The men are not privy to this.* **Mina** *is not really in the room with them. This is* **Mina**'s *last moments in her mind with* **Lucy***.*

Mina   For she contained more than they had ever known. They did not know of the night-time whispers where we confessed our desires. Strong feelings we didn't understand. Urges from the core of us. Together we would try and decipher what they meant.

They hold onto each other.

And why no one had warned us of them. And how we were supposed to achieve them when it seemed that we were not supposed to have them. We were able to answer questions for each other. We spoke a language only we knew. We kept secret our needs from the world but together we held them for each other because deep down I think we both knew how they weren't just something to be ignored.

Lucy *is dead.* **Mina** *stands away from her. The men cover her in a sheet and leave.* **Mina** *goes to her and sits on her bed.*

Mina   And for my friend it seemed that she had somehow opened herself up to her fears and in so doing it had killed her. I wish I had been able to tell her what I know now. Because I miss her, so much.

Mina *steps away from the bed and* **Lucy** *is whisked away.*

BLOOFER LADY

Mina   By now Jonathan and I had arrived in London. And the first thing that happened was that Jonathan saw him.

Jonathan   Walking down Piccadilly. As bold as brass. There he was.

Mina   He did not recognise him at first because he had changed so much. He was suddenly so much younger. Though his features were the same. His boldness, his ability to be out in public, it showed us how his strength had grown. We went to see Van Helsing.

Van Helsing   Mina, my dear. Your letter was timely. I'm only sorry I was unable to save your friend.

Mina   I fear that she was too far gone before you arrived.

Van Helsing   Perhaps. However, I should have seen the signs much earlier. And now it is imperative I complete what must be done.

Mina   What do you mean?

Van Helsing   There have been sightings.

Mina   Of what?

Van Helsing   They call her the Bloofer Lady.

Mina *laughs.*

Mina   The what?

Van Helsing   The Bloofer Lady.

Mina *laughs.*

Van Helsing   Yes, alright, I know. It is a childish way to describe a beautiful lady.

Mina   Childish?

Van Helsing   I'm afraid that's who she preys on. Here –

He gives them a newspaper each.

Jonathan (*reading*)   '*During the past two or three days several cases have occurred of young children straying from home or neglecting to return from their playing on the Heath . . .*' It continues '*The consensus of their excuses is that they had been with a "bloofer lady".*'

Mina (*reading*)   '*Some have been slightly torn or wounded in the throat . . .*'

Jonathan   Is it him?

Van Helsing   Perhaps.

Mina   Would he take the form of a woman?

Van Helsing   He is capable of anything.

Mina   But you think it is something else?

Van Helsing   I'm afraid I am worried it could be something much worse.

Jonathan   What could be worse than Dracula?

Van Helsing   His creation. I think the creature that is preying on the children is your dear friend – Lucy.

Mina   No!

Van Helsing   We will only be sure by exhuming her coffin. Tonight I will go there. If she is in her coffin then I will be proved wrong. If she is gone then. Well. God help us.

They all leave except **Mina**.

Mina   They would say that she was so beautiful and that she would ask for help. She would even promise sweets if they came with her. She would speak in a gentle voice and draw them towards her.

The figure of a woman, as before, stands with her back to us again. This time she does not turn and break the ominous vibe.

And every child had been told to not trust strangers. But this was a beautiful young lady. Surely she was no threat? Yes, perhaps if it had been a man they would have had their wits about them. But a woman like her? They felt safe.

The woman has gone.

And though the Heath had its many dark places, the kids knew which ones were to be avoided. They had grown up round here. They knew themselves. Perhaps she was truly lost. Perhaps if they helped her they would receive a reward. And didn't their parents always tell them to be good Samaritans? Didn't the Bible say as much?

An ominous sound is building.

So they would go towards her. Asking her if they could help. And she would smile and it would be so beautiful they could do nothing except get closer. As if drawn towards her by some invisible force they had no control over.

The woman emerges again but from a completely different place. She is in a long white gown and her face is concealed by her long straggly hair. When she walks it is with a slow jerkiness.

And as they got closer and closer, their eyes adjusting to the dark of the Heath – they would begin to see things they had not seen before. Her long hair was unkempt, straggling and knotty. Her white robe was torn and filthy. Her eyes had begun to glow red. Her hands seemed crooked, with long nails and fingers that trembled. And finally they would look to her mouth. As it opened in a terrible smile, they would see the jagged teeth just before she would sink them into their necks.

A scream and simultaneously the woman on stage disappears and several identical women appear in various parts of the auditorium.

Snap to black.

Lights up on **Mina** *again. The women have gone.*

Oh I was sure it was Lucy but they needed confirmation. So that night they went to her coffin.

The crypt. The men all approach **Lucy's** *closed coffin.*

Van Helsing   If I am right then she will not be in it.

They open the coffin with great difficulty. Finally the lid lifts.

Holmwood   It is empty! My Lucy!

Dr Seward   This only proves that she is not in the coffin. We need more proof than this that she is somehow doing something completely scientifically impossible.

Van Helsing   Very well. We will wait and watch for her.

Mina   And they did. In the dark of the cemetery they waited. Several hours passed with every tiny sound from animals and the wind making them start in fear. When suddenly.

There is movement at the back. Something sprints across, carrying something. It disappears.

Quincey   What was that?

He rushes off in pursuit. The woman runs back at a sprint, this time not carrying anything. The men yell out in fear.

Quincey *returns with the bundle of a child in his arms.*

Van Helsing   What have you got there?

Quincey   A child.

Van Helsing   Is he wounded?

Quincey   I think we got him in time.

In the darkness the woman appears.

Lucy   Is my husband near?

Holmwood   Lucy?

Van Helsing   Stay back, Arthur. Don't go to her.

Lucy   Come to me. Leave them and come to me. My arms are hungry for you.

Holmwood *begins to walk towards her.*

Van Helsing Arthur, do not approach!

Lucy We can rest together, my love.

Van Helsing My god, get hold of him.

The other men try to restrain **Holmwood** *but he pulls away and goes towards* **Lucy.**

Lucy You can have all that I have, if you come to me.

Van Helsing Get back, hell beast!

Van Helsing *jumps forward with a crucifix which makes* **Lucy** *recoil.* **Holmwood** *seems to be released from his urge to be near her.*

Van Helsing Arthur, I must do something to stop her that I fear you will not permit.

Holmwood What has happened to her?

Van Helsing She is not Lucy anymore. Do you understand that?

Holmwood I do.

Van Helsing Will you allow me to do what I need to do?

Holmwood Is that Lucy's body or a demon in her shape?

Van Helsing It is her body and yet not it. But when the un-dead become such, there comes with the change the curse of immortality; they cannot die but must go on age after age adding new victims and multiplying evils of the world. For all that die from the preying of the un-dead become themselves un-dead and prey on their kind. If we can destroy her then the children whose blood she sucks will be saved. They will go back to their play unknowing what has been. And most blessed of all – when this now un-dead be made to rest as true dead, then her soul shall again be free.

Holmwood Then it should be my hand that releases her.

Van Helsing Are you sure?

Holmwood   Tell me what I am to do and I shall not falter.

They ready themselves around the coffin where **Lucy** *has collapsed.*

Mina   My friend. My brilliant friend. Who had been both sullied and freed by what had happened – was to be freed *again*. But what of this freedom? And at what cost? She had become monstrous in their eyes. And her desire for the children's blood was a horror we can all agree. But there was something in her that I understood. Something that perhaps I myself desired too. And yet these men were about to take it from her in the most horrible way.

Holmwood *has a large wooden stake and mallet that* **Van Helsing** *has given him. His sleeves are rolled up and he is standing over her coffin.*

Mina   But she would not go easily. And she would make sure she would stain them with what they did forever. For her release was also in death and Lucy was not ready to die.

Holmwood *drives the stake into* **Lucy** *– a cacophony of animalistic screams from her, limbs flailing, teeth baring and blood. SO MUCH BLOOD. It gushes and spurts and covers all the men. It is a total blood bath. The Shining levels of blood.*

In the staging of this please remember that the depiction of violence against oppressed bodies should never be done for shock or entertainment. Find a way to do this that exposes the inherent cowardice and weakness of the men and gives power to **Lucy**.

When it is over they stand dripping in it.

Van Helsing   And so. She is free.

Mina   In one way, yes.

The men shuffle off leaving bloody foot prints.

I just wish I had got to her before they did.

She pauses a moment, looking out into the darkness.

Are you still out there?

No response.

I know you're here tonight. And I'm glad. That you've finally decided to return.

BEGINNING OF THE END

Mina Jonathan?

Jonathan *approaches.*

Mina Do you remember what happens next?

Jonathan It was Renfield, was it not? Dr Seward's patient. You visited him.

Mina Yes.

Jonathan It is just as you told it before.

Mina Before when?

Jonathan When I was. I don't know. When I was . . .

Mina You're coping admirably.

Jonathan *(surprised)* Thank you.

Mina I appreciate how quickly you have taken this on.

Jonathan It's important.

Mina It is.

Jonathan At least that is what I feel. But I don't fully know why.

Mina That will come. Are you happy to proceed?

Jonathan Yes.

Mina You had discovered where the consignment of coffins that had arrived on the Demeter had ended up.

Jonathan The old chapel in Carfax.

Mina   For some reason it was right next door to Dr Seward's asylum. Which is why I visited Renfield. Whilst you went to investigate the coffins, I saw him. Dr Seward had noticed a horrible connection between the ravings of his patient and the experiences of Lucy and Jonathan.

RENFIELD

Renfield *emerges from the darkness.* **Dr Seward** *shows* **Mina** *towards him.* **Renfield** *moves like a bug.*

Dr Seward   Mr Renfield, I have someone to see you.

Renfield   What a novelty.

Dr Seward   Mr Renfield, you will behave as a gentleman does to a lady. My friend, Mrs Harker, is here to observe. I trust you will be on your best behaviour.

Renfield   Of course.

Dr Seward   Perhaps you will tell Mrs Harker of the delusions you suffer from.

Renfield   I used to fancy that life was a positive and perpetual entity and that by consuming a multitude of live things one might indefinitely prolong life. The blood is the life – isn't that right, Doctor?

Mina   And have you found that to be true?

Renfield   Not for me. For I have not been blessed with that ability. My master has not yet come to me.

Mina   Who is your master?

Renfield   You know him.

Mina   And if he were to come then what would he do?

Renfield   I would hope that he would help me to become as he is.

Mina   Why do you desire eternal life?

Renfield   No no, not eternal life. Eternal *love*.

Mina   What do you mean?

Renfield   It is love that he seeks.

Mina   You wish to tell me that in all his destruction and harm and pain and terror and fear – he is seeking love?

Renfield   Of course.

Mina   I won't believe it. I won't pity him. He took my friend from me. He tried to take my fiancé.

Renfield   And he will take you too.

Mina   What?

Renfield   But you will know love.

Mina   I do know love.

Renfield   Not like this. Not like his.

Mina   I don't understand.

Renfield   The pursuit of it is what defines you. He has chosen one way. Perhaps I would choose another. You . . .?

He looks at her and his face lights up.

The blood is the life, Mina, but the reason is love.

Dr Seward   We should go.

He pulls **Mina** *away.*

Renfield   I pray I do not see your sweet face again. But if I do – please release me too.

Dr Seward   He is quite mad. You must not heed a word he says.

Both **Renfield** *and* **Dr Seward** *go.*

Mina   Renfield would die soon. They would discover that the boxes of earth in the chapel did not contain the Count. Rats would swarm. Horrors would occur. And one night.

Finally. When I was alone. Whilst Jonathan was out with the men, hunting him. It would be my turn to be prey.

A distinct change in tone. She is in her own nightmare now.

Mina *is in bed. It is quiet. She sleeps. Suddenly the form of a man begins to emerge and crawl towards her bed.*

She wakes suddenly.

Who's there?

Voice   Do you remember me? Little Mina, what are you so scared of?

The man's limbs are long and strange. He continues to get closer and closer. We never see his face. We never see much of him.

If you do not face your fear it will destroy you. You must face me.

Mina   Who are you?

Voice   Do you not remember? The creature in the night. Visiting you. You thought he would protect you but he couldn't. His needs grew stronger than yours.

Mina   No.

The man has reached the bed and climbs up onto it and over **Mina**.

Voice   Little Mina, so scared. Let me look into your eyes. Let me feed on that terror. My power comes from your fear.

Mina   No!

The man goes to her neck and bites and feeds. She cries out but doesn't resist. When he pulls away he looks down on her.

Voice   You have a choice to make now.

Mina   Is it a choice?

Voice   It is an inevitability. But you can take it willingly or not. Flesh of my flesh. Blood of my blood.

Mina   What did my friend do?

Voice   Oh, she resisted. She had to be forced. But that was also her desire.

Mina *reacts angrily to this, pushing him away.*

Mina   How could you?

He laughs.

Voice   This is a brilliant scene. You are a great actor. Your facade it convincing but with my power comes my ability to see your true desires. You do not have to pretend with me anymore. Drink.

He uses a nail to open his skin on his neck and then takes her head and pulls her to it. She drinks.

The people step on stage and watch this. When she is done she falls back on the bed. He disappears. She looks up at the people.

She wipes her hand across her mouth to remove the blood. She looks around at her people then springs into action.

THE HUNT

Mina   Jonathan. Take it.

Jonathan   He escaped. Back in his ship to Varna. We knew that if we didn't pursue him he could return any time. Renewed. More powerful than before. I wanted to leave Mina.

Mina   I was a 'vulnerable woman', but I would prove invaluable.

Jonathan   For she was now connected to him. His dreams were her dreams.

Van Helsing   What do you see now, Mina?

Mina   There is the sound of men stamping overhead, creaking of chains and I'm still. So very still. It feels like death somehow.

Van Helsing   Do you hear the water against the side of the ship?

Mina   Yes.

Van Helsing   He still sails.

Mina   I was worried that my need for him would overwhelm me. That I would do something to the men.

Jonathan   But she needn't have worried. We all promised that at the first sign of transformation we would destroy her like we did Lucy. We travelled as fast as we could. In pursuit.

Van Helsing   Where is he now?

Mina   The waves are no longer lapping. I hear men's voices. They are moving him onto land.

Van Helsing   We must get ahead of him.

Mina   Trains, carriages. We travelled. I dreamed. I dreamed of the Demeter. I dreamt that I killed all those men and tossed them into the sea. I dreamt of all he drank from and destroyed. I dreamt of Lucy. My Lucy. I saw what he did to her. And my anger grew.

Jonathan   Where is he now, my love?

Mina   Horses, shouts. He is being transported on a track. Wolves in the distance.

Jonathan   Oh god.

Mina   What is it?

Jonathan   The wolves are his.

Mina   Is he close to his castle?

Van Helsing   Not as close as us I hope.

Mina   We arrived at Castle Dracula. It was just as Jonathan had described it in his journal. No lights. No welcoming warmth. Just cold grey walls and dark windows for eyes. When we entered it was with trepidation.

CASTLE DRACULA

Mina   It was then that we heard the horses. The carriage with Dracula's coffin had arrived.

The three creatures emerge. Large and terrifying. They come towards them.

Creature   Come to us, Mina. Come, sister. You are ours now.

Mina   I wanted to. So much. But –

The men yell a battle cry and they fight the creatures. One by one they sever their heads until they are destroyed. More blood.

It was then that we heard the horses. The carriage with Dracula's coffin had arrived.

Van Helsing   Hold steady now. He will emerge. And he will not expect that we are here.

Mina   How could he not? I was here. We were, after all, connected.

We do not see Dracula but we hear him.

Voice   Welcome, my friends.

Holmwood   We are no friend to you! Show yourself, beast!

Voice   It takes great bravery to come to my home like this.

Quincey   We out number you.

Voice   Incorrect. I am many. You are in grave danger.

The sound of wolves.

Van Helsing   You do not scare us.

Voice   Hello, Mina. I have enjoyed being in your dreams.

Jonathan   Leave her alone.

Voice   Don't worry. She is more than capable of defending herself. Aren't you, Mina?

Jonathan   Show yourself, devil, and let this be a fair fight!

Voice   This will never be fair. And yet perhaps it will be what it needs to be. Are you ready? Then we shall begin.

What follows is a fight with something we can't see. However, we see the blows the men receive. They are lifted and thrown. They are attacked by an invisible force. It seems an impossible thing to defeat.

They are weakened and losing and **Quincey** *in particular is badly injured when his own sword turns on him and impales him.*

It is only when **Mina** *steps into the middle of it and holding up her hand manages to grab something by the throat. In grabbing it, it materialises – it is Dracula.*

With her other hand she impales him with a stake.

Dracula   Thank you.

He crumbles to nothing and disappears.

Mina *stands amongst the groaning men, all badly beaten up. She goes to* **Quincey** *who is dying.*

It begins to snow.

Quincey   Is he gone?

Mina   He is.

Quincey   Oh god, it was worth this to die. Look – the sun is rising.

The sun rises. The snow mixes with the blood.

END

Mina *looks to everyone and nods. They disappear, leaving only* **Jonathan**.

Mina   When we returned home you gave me the greatest love I could have asked for. Our child.

Jonathan   We named him after Quincey.

Mina   Flesh of my flesh. Blood of my blood.

Jonathan   The future.

Mina   Yes, my darling. He was. And he lived a good life. A long life. Untroubled by what troubled us.

Jonathan   A long life?

Mina   Yes. I was never going to allow my child to suffer. It was so long ago now but he died an old man. Unlike you.

Jonathan   Me?

Mina   Ah yes, there it is. There in your eyes. Very similar to Jonathan actually. Disappointment. Shock. When you realise the truth. When he realised the truth. That after everything we went through it would end up like this. That this was all he would ever amount to. All you would amount to. And having that choice taken from his hands was so unfamiliar to him. To have your agency so cruelly ripped away was what one would expect from a creature like the Count. Not from the person he loved. Not from the person who had helped him destroy his tormentor. Such an unexpected sensation. I love to see that appear in their eyes as it all dawns on them.

Jonathan   Wait.

Mina   Yes?

Jonathan   You're speaking of Jonathan and I like we are the same.

Mina   Well spotted.

Jonathan   But I know I'm not truly Jonathan.

Mina   You are correct again. You are not Jonathan.

Jonathan   So.

Mina   So.

Jonathan   Who am I?

Mina   It is always around now where I let a little of their consciousness slide back in. A moment or so. A flicker. Like the memory of a dream that you grasp at before it slips away forever. Think a little harder. You're almost there. Tell them. Who are you?

Jonathan   Oh god.

Mina   Yes?

Jonathan   I remember now.

Mina   What do you remember?

Jonathan   Yes.

Mina   Tell them.

Jonathan   I was there. Out there.

He points out to the audience.

Just last night.

Mina   You were.

Jonathan   What is this? What have you done to me? I was watching. Like them. I came with my family. Where are they now? Are they still there? How did you do this to me? Oh god.

He shouts out to us.

Run. Run now if you can. She will take you. Like she has me. She will take you. My god RUN. Go! Get out of here! RUN!

Mina *has calmly approached him as he shouts.*

Mina   Sleep now.

In one swift movement she breaks his neck and he falls to the ground.

She waits and watches as some of her people, her acolytes, come and drag him away.

Everyone except **Mina** *has gone. She stands covered in blood and commanding of the space. She calls out.*

Mina   Lucy? You're here, aren't you?

No answer at first then a strange sound that makes **Mina** *look in its direction.*

Why now? All this time and you choose tonight.

A spike of a sound that could be a voice, a whisper, imperceptible. It comes from a different direction. **Mina** *looks.*

Are you here to stop me? Or to help? In all the years since you've been gone, I have watched their fear grow. It's too much now. Is that why?

Another sound, louder than before. Startling. **Mina** *smiles.*

Then we'll do this together. Tonight. It's time.

A deep low hum can be imperceptibly heard. It builds over the following. She turns her attention to the audience.

I find it curious that Jonathan's account of these events seem to omit my own transformation. As if he was too scared to write of it. It was implied I was safe when I was not. Of course I wasn't. I drank the blood after all. And that wasn't the end for me.

The blood is the life. The reason is love.

When Dracula was released from his curse there was such a look of relief upon his face before he became dust. He had been tied to this beast, enslaved as much as us. It was in that moment I knew that what he had been infected with was not evil. It was pure love. Pure, undiluted love. Where need and desire and want mix so strongly that there is nothing you can do to control yourself. But his love became monstrous. He was too weak to control it. It was too big for him.

The people who have aided her presentation start to creep on the stage behind her, they are her army of vampires.

She looks at them and smiles.

But it's not too big for us.

She points at each vampire as she speaks:

Lu Ming, freed from a life of pain and servitude in 1899. Elsie, freed from a family who could not accept them in 1928. Margaret Grace, freed from a monstrous husband in 1952. Danny, freed from a horrific assault in 1996.There are thousands more. All freed. By me. And each other.

She looks back at the audience.

I could free you too. If you like? You see fear, like shame, is something that should switch allegiances. We fear their wrath, we fear the monsters they tell us of to distract us from their own crimes, we fear their punishment, we fear their disdain, we fear their disgust, we fear their violence. But it is clear that so many of us are the monsters in *their* woods. For they know what we would do with the power they hold if we got it. It is not us that is scared, it is them. So why not give them something to be truly scared of?

The vampires have slipped away.

This is our world now.

Tonight I will come to one man in the audience and you will join us for the next presentation.

My next Jonathan.

She looks around the auditorium.

Someone who has forsaken his family perhaps. His partner. Maybe someone who has used his power to belittle and demean. Someone who knows what they have done and will do it again. There is always somebody. Everywhere we go.

She smiles, satisfied.

I have chosen. You will know who you are soon enough. But do not be scared. Your role in all this is a noble one. A chance to redeem yourself. And don't worry, you won't really feel a thing.

And I will also come for those of you who are ready to be free. Those ready to join me. I already feel so many of you calling for me.

Because I know you are weary of this world and those within it that have harmed you so greatly. And you are angry. Aren't you? And you should be.

But now they will see that their violence taught us something about the violence we will do to them. And before they breathe their last they will know the fear we have known our whole lives. And when they have all gone? We will start again. With only our love.

So when the blood comes. And the fear and the horror. Keep reminding yourselves – the reason is love.

Tonight.

When you go to sleep. When I come to you. And I will come to you.

I will offer you our riddle. Our question. And this is your chance to free yourselves. For Lucy. This is your chance to choose the wolf, my darlings. No fear anymore. Stand strong in the power that is coming to you. Raise your chin. Bare your neck. And choose the wolf.

A horrible scream. The vampires are all in the auditorium for this, close to the audience. Black out. Snap back up and she and the vampires are gone.

The End.

Methuen Drama Modern Plays

include

Bola Agbaje
Ayad Akhtar
Edward Albee
Jean Anouilh
John Arden
Peter Barnes
Clare Barron
Sebastian Barry
Alistair Beaton
Brendan Behan
Edward Bond
William Boyd
Bertolt Brecht
Howard Brenton
Amelia Bullmore
Anthony Burgess
Leo Butler
Jim Cartwright
Lolita Chakrabarti
Caryl Churchill
Lucinda Coxon
Tim Crouch
Shelagh Delaney
Ishy Din
Claire Dowie
David Edgar
David Eldridge
Dario Fo
Michael Frayn
John Godber
James Graham
David Greig
John Guare
Lauren Gunderson
Peter Handke
David Harrower
Jonathan Harvey
Robert Holman
David Ireland
Sarah Kane

Barrie Keeffe
Jasmine Lee-Jones
Anders Lustgarten
Duncan Macmillan
David Mamet
Patrick Marber
Martin McDonagh
Alistair McDowall
Arthur Miller
Tom Murphy
Phyllis Nagy
Anthony Neilson
Peter Nichols
Ben Okri
Joe Orton
Vinay Patel
Joe Penhall
Luigi Pirandello
Stephen Poliakoff
Lucy Prebble
Peter Quilter
Mark Ravenhill
Philip Ridley
Willy Russell
Sam Shepard
Martin Sherman
Chris Shinn
Jackie Sibblies Drury
Wole Soyinka
Simon Stephens
Kae Tempest
Laura Wade
Anne Washburn
Timberlake Wertenbaker
Roy Williams
Snoo Wilson
Theatre Workshop
Frances Ya-Chu Cowhig
Benjamin Zephaniah

Methuen Drama Contemporary Dramatists

include

John Arden (two volumes)
Arden & D'Arcy
Peter Barnes (three volumes)
Sebastian Barry
Mike Bartlett
Clare Barron
Brad Birch
Dermot Bolger
Edward Bond (ten volumes)
Howard Brenton (two volumes)
Leo Butler (two volumes)
Richard Cameron
Jim Cartwright
Caryl Churchill (two volumes)
Complicite
Sarah Daniels (two volumes)
Nick Darke
David Edgar (three volumes)
David Eldridge (two volumes)
Ben Elton
Per Olov Enquist
Dario Fo (two volumes)
Michael Frayn (four volumes)
John Godber (four volumes)
Paul Godfrey
James Graham (two volumes)
David Greig
John Guare
Lee Hall (two volumes)
Katori Hall
Peter Handke
Jonathan Harvey (two volumes)
Iain Heggie
Israel Horovitz
Declan Hughes
Terry Johnson (three volumes)
Sarah Kane
Barrie Keeffe
Bernard-Marie Koltès (two volumes)
Franz Xaver Kroetz
Kwame Kwei-Armah
David Lan
Bryony Lavery
Deborah Levy
Doug Lucie

Alistair MacDowall
Sabrina Mahfouz
David Mamet (six volumes)
Patrick Marber
Martin McDonagh
Duncan McLean
David Mercer (two volumes)
Anthony Minghella (two volumes)
Rory Mullarkey
Tom Murphy (six volumes)
Phyllis Nagy
Anthony Neilson (three volumes)
Peter Nichol (two volumes)
Philip Osment
Gary Owen
Louise Page
Stewart Parker (two volumes)
Joe Penhall (two volumes)
Stephen Poliakoff (three volumes)
David Rabe (two volumes)
Mark Ravenhill (three volumes)
Christina Reid
Philip Ridley (two volumes)
Willy Russell
Eric-Emmanuel Schmitt
Ntozake Shange
Sam Shepard (two volumes)
Martin Sherman (two volumes)
Christopher Shinn (two volumes)
Joshua Sobel
Wole Soyinka (two volumes)
Simon Stephens (five volumes)
Shelagh Stephenson
David Storey (three volumes)
C. P. Taylor
Sue Townsend
Judy Upton (two volumes)
Michel Vinaver (two volumes)
Arnold Wesker (two volumes)
Peter Whelan
Michael Wilcox
Roy Williams (four volumes)
David Williamson
Snoo Wilson (two volumes)
David Wood (two volumes)
Victoria Wood

For a complete listing of
Methuen Drama titles, visit:
www.bloomsbury.com/drama

Follow us on X and keep up to date with
our news and publications
@MethuenDrama